J 304.2 Kel
Kelsey, Elin
Not your typical book about the
environment /

34028074144230
MM $10.95 ocn455790604
        09/14/10

3 4028 07414 4230
HARRIS COUNTY PUBLIC LIBRARY

W9-DDX-346

NOT YOUR TYPICAL BOOK ABOUT THE ENVIRONMENT

ELIN KELSEY

Illustrated by
Clayton Hanmer

WITHDRAWN

Owlkids Books Inc.
10 Lower Spadina Avenue, Suite 400, Toronto, Ontario M5V 2Z2
www.owlkids.com

Text © 2010 Elin Kelsey
Illustrations © 2010 Clayton Hanmer

All rights reserved. No part of this book may be reproduced or copied
in any form without written consent from the publisher.

Distributed in Canada by Raincoast Books
9050 Shaughnessy Street, Vancouver, British Columbia V6P 6E5

Distributed in the United States by Publishers Group West
1700 Fourth Street, Berkeley, California 94710

Library and Archives Canada Cataloguing in Publication

Kelsey, Elin
        Not your typical book about the environment / Elin Kelsey, Clayton Hanmer.

Includes index.
ISBN 978-1-897349-79-3 (bound).--ISBN 978-1-897349-84-7 (pbk.)

        1. Human ecology--Juvenile literature. 2. Sustainable living--Juvenile
literature. I. Hanmer, Clayton, 1978- II. Title.

GF48.K45 2010   j304.2   C2009-905896-0

Library of Congress Control Number: 2009937493

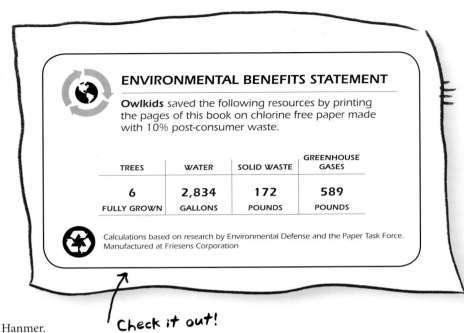

Check it out!

ENVIRONMENTAL BENEFITS STATEMENT

Owlkids saved the following resources by printing the pages of this book on chlorine free paper made with 10% post-consumer waste.

TREES	WATER	SOLID WASTE	GREENHOUSE GASES
6 FULLY GROWN	2,834 GALLONS	172 POUNDS	589 POUNDS

Calculations based on research by Environmental Defense and the Paper Task Force. Manufactured at Friesens Corporation

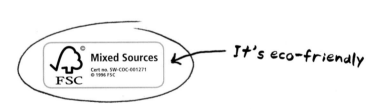

Mixed Sources
Cert no. SW-COC-001271
© 1996 FSC
FSC

It's eco-friendly

Canada Council Conseil des Arts
for the Arts   du Canada

ONTARIO ARTS COUNCIL
CONSEIL DES ARTS DE L'ONTARIO

We acknowledge the financial support of the Canada Council for the Arts, the Ontario Arts Council, the Government of
Canada through the Book Publishing Industry Development Program (BPIDP), and the Government of Ontario through the
Ontario Media Development Corporation's Book Initiative for our publishing activities.

Manufactured by Friesens Corporation
Manufactured in Altona, Manitoba, Canada, in January 2010
Job #52617

A   B   C   D   E   F

Publisher of Chirp, chickaDEE and OWL
www.owlkids.com

p4 Introduction

p6 Chapter One
Fast Fashion
How your clothing is changing to suit a cleaner world

p20 Chapter Two
Hungry Planet
Finding ways to feed ourselves... without starving our planet

p36 Chapter Three
Techno Planet
How new gadgets both help and hurt the Earth

p48 Chapter Four
People Power
From the steps you take to the waste you make... YOU are energy

Index p64

For Kip, Esmé, Katherine, James, Matthias, Lucas, Alanna, Fiona, Marielle, and Sylvie

WARNING:
THIS IS NOT A TYPICAL BOOK ABOUT THE ENVIRONMENT!

It is not filled with doom-and-gloom messages about the state of the planet. It does not blame you, your baby sister, or your uncle Irving for climate change. It will not introduce huge, gnarly problems that are too big to deal with. Oh yeah, the word "extinction" barely shows up at all. In fact, there's a good chance that reading this book will make you feel hopeful...maybe even happy.

No kidding. Happy. A book about the environment that makes you feel happy? Whodathunkit?

My name is Elin, *and I wrote this book for everyone who loves the countless wonderful things about living on Earth—from the simple stuff like swimming in the ocean or the year's first snowfall to the thrill of discovering surprising new ideas. I wrote it because no matter where you look, you're bombarded with these hopeless messages about the future of our planet. I wanted to write a hopeful book about the environment.*

Here's the thing—all that doom-and-gloom stuff is only half the story. You are not nature's bogeyman. You *are* nature. You're connected to this great wide world in ways beyond your wildest imagination. The feathers in your pillow likely grew on the breast of a duck raised in China. The foam in your stuffed animals was made from 400-million-year-old remains of microscopic plants and animals buried deep within the Earth. The air that you breathe is alive with teeny-tiny insects, seeds, and the pollen from more than 100,000 species of flowering plants. All these connections mean that you have power.

What power? Well, the power to choose! What you wear, how you get to school, what you eat—infinite possibilities exist about the ways you can choose to live. According to happiness researchers (believe it or not, there are people in universities studying what makes us happy!), these choices can make you, other people, and the millions of animals and plants on Earth much happier. Inside these pages, you'll discover how your favorite video game touches the lives of African gorillas, how soda bottles can morph into your cozy fleece hoodie, and how a bike can grow in your backyard. It all depends on how you envision your world.

Ready to explore the remarkable connections between you and everything else on Earth?
Turn the page!

Chapter One

FAST FASHION

It's time to slow down!

Is that the time? You're going to be late! You drag yourself from the warmth of your bed and yank open your drawers.

Hey! What happened here? Inside, you find tufts of silky white fibers as soft as bunny tails hanging from stalks where your jeans and T-shirts should be! And what's this? Thick, slippery oil pools in the bottom of your sock drawer and drips from the hangers in your closet. Where are your clothes?

You don't usually see it so dramatically, but your clothing comes from things that were once alive. T-shirts and jeans begin their lives as cotton growing in places like India or the southern United States. Socks, bathing suits, shirts, fuzzy pajamas, and jackets contain atoms from tiny aquatic organisms that swam in a prehistoric sea. Between their birth and the shopping mall, those microscopic life forms died, were buried by mud, and eventually got squeezed and cooked into petroleum deep within the Earth. Hundreds of millions of years later, we humans pump this "black gold" up to the surface and deliver it to refineries, where it is processed into synthetic fabrics like acrylic and polyester. Half the fabric on Earth today is made from petroleum-based chemicals.

Every year, humans collectively spend one thousand billion dollars on clothes. And more than two-thirds of all that money comes from shoppers just in the United States, Canada, and Western Europe—that's a very small part of the world's population. You probably own a lot more clothes than your parents did when they were kids. You could balance an adult golden retriever against the average weight of the clothes each kid in your class buys in a year. What's in style changes faster and the temptation to buy is far greater than ever before. You see more ads in a day than your great-grandparents saw in their whole lives!

But just as too much cheap fast food isn't good for your body, too much cheap fast fashion isn't good for the Earth. All those throwaway fashions gobble up raw materials faster than the planet can replenish them and guzzle oil that can never be replaced. Plus, to make clothes so cheaply, companies may cut corners on environmental safety or underpay the people who grow and produce their materials. Trouble is, you can't see these negatives because there are so many steps between the crop, the fiber, the factory, the transporter, the distributor, and the store. You're just looking for a new shirt.

Before all these concerns about clothing lead to thoughts of going without (brrrrrrr!), consider this: Experts all over the world are inventing safer, healthier materials for clothing— and transforming the clothing we no longer wear in ways you never imagined! *So slip into something comfortable and turn the page…*

HOW THIRSTY ARE YOUR CLOTHES?

How do we make everyone's wardrobe as eco-friendly as it is fashionable?

Great style, color, comfort, price—the last thing you think about when you're shopping is how much your clothes drink. But many of your favorite clothes have an almost unquenchable thirst. Nearly 2.5 billion T-shirts are sold on Earth each year. Unlike synthetic fabrics such as fleece, the fibers in your 100% cotton T-shirts and denim jeans were grown, not manufactured. Conventionally grown cotton is intensively farmed to get the highest yield (that's the biggest harvest for the smallest unit of land). And that cotton is one thirsty plant. It takes twenty-five bathtubs of water to grow enough cotton for one lonely T-shirt. It also takes lots of oil to power heavy farm machinery and make fertilizers. Plus, even more oil is needed to create the astonishing amounts of human-made chemical pesticides used to prevent insects, mice, and other animals from damaging the crops.

The "perfect" T-shirt

With an eye for finding greener options, designers have launched a contest to create the "perfect" T-shirt, made from materials that do as little harm to the planet as possible. Which would you choose to wear? Let's meet the contestants!

T-shirt A: *Bamboo*

This plant grows like Jack's beanstalk, reaching adult size in three or four years without the aid of pesticides. It requires much less water than cotton and can even survive droughts.

But: Critics say the processes needed to turn bamboo into soft T-shirts require lots of nasty toxic chemicals.

T-shirt B: *Hemp*

Hemp also grows very quickly, and it needs much less water and land to grow than cotton.

But: Critics feel hemp should not be grown because it's a cousin of marijuana. Industrial hemp is legal in Canada, parts of Europe, China, India...but currently not the United States.

T-shirt C: *Organic cotton*

Fans love it because some organic cotton is rain-fed, not irrigated, so it may use less water than conventional cotton. Organic farmers can only use chemicals derived from natural sources, such as plants and minerals, to fertilize their crops or protect them from pests. Organic farming involves crop rotation, which enriches the soil and provides habitats for wild birds, bees, and other animals.

But: Critics argue that organic cotton has a lower yield, so more natural habitat must be cleared to grow the same number of shirts. And each shirt is more expensive. They say organic doesn't necessarily mean pesticide-free. Plus, many of the natural chemicals organic farmers use are still toxic.

T-shirt D: *Vintage*

Buying vintage tees from a thrift store is a perfect way to avoid the costs of making new T-shirts—the shirts are already made! Plus, they're affordable, unique, and great-looking to boot.

But: Critics say, "I want new!"

How eco-friendly is your closet?

Being lean and green in your closet isn't so hard—chances are, you're already doing more than you know. Go ahead and give yourself points for:

- having hand-me-downs or thrift-store buys
- having things you've worn for more than a year
- borrowing a ski jacket or snorkel for a vacation rather than buying a new one you'll rarely use
- not washing your clothes after each wear
- drying your clothes on a clothesline
- having an item made from an environmentally friendly fabric
- having something that has been mended
- getting your clothes dirty by playing outside
- donating stained or worn-out clothes to a company that makes rags

Keeping your clothes green and clean

Most of the electricity used by washing machines goes to just heating the water. Every time you (or that person who does all that wash...oh yeah, your mom!) set the temperature on COLD the whole world benefits. If North Americans washed their clothes in cold water, it would reduce carbon emissions by as much as taking 10 million cars off the road each year.

Many neighborhoods banned clotheslines because people thought they were ugly. Today, governments are reducing carbon emissions by restoring people's rights to air laundry in public. Hasta la vista, you energy-sucking clothesdryers!

ECO-FABRICS ARE SPROUTING UP EVERYWHERE!

Green Glam

Not long ago, eco-fashion meant organic cotton yoga pants and saggy hemp T-shirts. Today, major labels like Versace, Diesel, and Stella McCartney, as well as smaller niche designers, are creating greener glam. They use more sustainable natural fibers like bamboo, or newly created fabrics like lyocell, a soft fiber made from sustainably forested wood pulp and recycled paper.

A Fiber of a Different Feather

Chemists may not be the people you'd imagine at a fashion show, but they're at the heart of the recent explosion of new eco-fabrics. Driven by a need to find less toxic, renewable alternatives to synthetic fibers and cotton, chemists are making textiles from some unexpected sources. A team of chemists in Nebraska, for instance, has developed a special combination of chemicals and enzymes to produce fibers from chicken feathers that will resemble wool and a rice straw fabric with the look and feel of cotton. With millions of tons of waste chicken feathers and rice straw available from poultry farms worldwide each year, such innovations could turn out to be the goose that laid the golden egg.

Airplane food

Soy, banana, bamboo shoots, and vegetables...many eco-friendly fabrics sound good enough to eat. In fact, you could eat the fabric on the seats of some Lufthansa airplanes. The evolution of this remarkable fabric began when the Swiss government insisted that leftover textile trimmings be treated as toxic waste because they contained so many dangerous chemicals.

Rather than going the expensive route of hazardous waste disposal or the less ethical route of moving to another country where the requirements for environmental protection and human health are not so high, fabric company Rohner Textil AG created a third option. They designed an eco-fabric that wasn't toxic in the first place! They had to change many things, from the source of their raw materials to how their factory operates, but they were so successful that the water they use in production is now cleaner when it leaves the facility than when it first enters it! Though their new eco-fabric isn't designed to be food, it ends up being safe enough to eat.

Elin Explains

HOW SEA OTTERS ARE CONNECTED TO FISH STICKS

What does historic fashion have to do with the food in your freezer?
Find out how!

faux fur hat

1700s – 1800s: Wealthy people love to wear fancy fur hats, collars, and cuffs.

1750 – 1800s: Lots of sea otters lure fur traders to the west coast of North America.

1750 – 1800s: Fur traders make mucho $$$...but sea otter population drops from 300,000 to 2,000.

1911: International treaty against killing sea otters. Fur falls out of fashion.

Slowly, sea otters return to parts of their historic range in Canada, the United States, and Russia.

Today: Sea otters eat urchins and other invertebrates that feed on kelp, so kelp forests flourish.

Kelp forests provide underwater nurseries for baby fish.

Baby fish become bigger fish that are eaten by predatory fish like white hake.

Fishers catch white hake.

White hake and other fish become fish sticks in the box in your freezer.

Overfishing of white hake and other fish means less food for sea lions and seals. As sea lion and seal numbers drop, killer whales that once fed upon them switch to eating sea otters.

But you know a way to help the white hake and sea otters!

You download the Seafood Watch program's list of sustainable seafood choices to your cell phone…
www.montereybayaquarium.org/cr/seafoodwatch.aspx

…and choose sustainable fish—like Pacific halibut—for your fish and chips instead! They're caught in ways the ocean can sustain so that sea otters and killer whales can live healthy lives!

Invite a sea otter out for a seafood dinner… but be sure NOT to wear a fur hat!

ARE BOTTLES FOR DRINKING...OR WEARING?

You do the math!

Plastic bottles. They're everywhere, holding everything from soda to juice to water to cleaning products. And when you recycle a bottle, it becomes another bottle, right? Not always—in fact, you might be wearing someone's old root beer bottle right now! Let's do some math together...

25 plastic bottles = 1 new fleece jacket

If they're lucky, the plastic bottles in your recycling bin will end up as a polyester fleece jacket. Like soda bottles, synthetic clothes are essentially plastic and are made from petroleum-based polymers. Polymers are large molecules made of little repeated chemical units—kind of like beads on a string. Bottles can be chopped up into flakes, cleaned, dried, and melted. The melted plastic is then squeezed into long strands of fiber, which are spun into yarn and woven to make your snuggly fleece.

1 old fleece jacket + few bottles = 1 new fleece jacket

The great thing about fleece is that once it wears out it can be recycled again into a brand-new jacket. A growing number of fabric manufacturers specialize in recycled fibers. So when your old fleece is too worn out to pass along to a younger cousin, drop it off at Mountain Equipment Co-op, Patagonia, or another store with a recycling program. They'll send it off to be turned back into basic polyester, combined with newer material, and stretched into synthetic fibers. TA-DA! It's a new fleece jacket.

A leading British supermarket chain was the first to create a fashionable line of shirts, pants, and skirts made from plastic bags, food packaging, and even meat trays that their stores normally throw away!

150 fleece jackets SAVES 1 barrel of oil

If Only a quarter of all plastic bottles in North America are currently recycled. Every time you rescue a plastic bottle by putting it into a recycling bin, you reduce the amount of energy, waste, pollution, and greenhouse gases needed to make plastic from raw petroleum. That's important because oil is a non-renewable resource. Unlike trees which can grow again from seeds, oil is gone for good once it's used up.

Fish and sea turtles say thanks!

Marine animals benefit when you shop with a canvas bag. Why? Because it's one less plastic bag that can end up in the ocean—in whole or in pieces. Plastic manufacturers ship 235 million metric tonnes (260 million tons) of tiny plastic pellets called nurdles to factories around the world each year. As small and light as lentils, nurdles easily escape from shipping containers and are blown into the sea. Unfortunately, fish and seabirds often gobble them up, mistaking the nurdles for bits of plankton or fish eggs. In many sad cases, these animals starve to death because there is no room for food in bellies stuffed with plastic.

"No" works in any language

Every time you say no to a plastic bag you are sending a message, and it's being heard. From Taiwan and Bangladesh to Ireland and Thailand, a growing wave of places around the world are banning or charging taxes on non-recyclable plastic bags. In 2008, the Chinese government prohibited all stores from offering plastic bags for free. In one year, the 1.3 billion people in China used 40 billion fewer "bags and saved the 1.45 million tonnes (1.6 million tons) of petroleum it would have used to make them.

FROM GARBAGE TO GREAT!

Wanna punk up your junk? There's lots of ways to make good on your garbage.

Re-use industries that make new things from garbage are springing up around the world. Whether it's food waste, old clothes, or even animal by-products, they're taking all the stuff that we no longer need and turning it into surprising products. *Take a look!*

coconut husks = nets to
prevent soil erosion
(Philippines)

salmon skin = bikinis
(Chile)

blue jeans = house insulation
(United States)

pig urine = plastic plates
(Denmark)

Heh heh

Munch Munch

plastic bags = railroad ties
(United Kingdom)

BAGS

ECO FRESH

HANDBAGS

vinyl billboards = purses
(Colombia)

kitchen waste = gardens
(Around the world)

compost

sand = pearls
(That's right—oysters from oceans around the world have been in on the act for ages!)

Hubba Hubba!

Well, I never!

It's a shoe-in!

When your favorite running shoes are too ragged and smelly to share with others, consider donating them to Nike's Reuse-A-Shoe program. Since they first started collecting worn-out athletic shoes (they'll accept any brand), Nike has recycled more than 22 million pairs. The sneakers are sliced into three sections, then ground up into their component materials: rubber from the outsole, foam from the midsole, and fabric from the shoe's upper. The rubber is used to create soccer and football fields. The foam is used for tennis courts. The fabric becomes the padding under hardwood basketball floors. Take a look at how many shoes it takes to make these fun places to play:

- *Basketball court:* 2,500 pairs

- *Tennis court:* 2,500 pairs

- *Full field or soccer pitch:* 50,000 to 75,000 pairs

- *Running track:* 75,000 pairs

- *Playground:* 2,500 pairs

INSPIRED BY NATURE

Using nature's genius to design better clothes, buildings, machines, and much more!

Bio·mim·ic·ry (noun)

Biomimicry is about using nature's best biological ideas to solve human problems. Or in other words, asking, "What would nature do?" Humans may have a long way to go toward living sustainably on this planet, but the 5 to 100 million species we share the Earth with have the time-tested genius to help us get there.

When you look at a forest, what do you see? A bunch of trees? A source of wood? How about a way to rethink the whole idea of trash? It's most common to make cradle-to-grave products that are dumped in landfills at the ends of their lives, but a growing number of companies are making products whose old parts can be turned into something new again. This cradle-to-cradle vision seeks to do away with the idea of trash entirely—it's an idea borrowed from nature. Old products become raw materials for new products, in much the same way that a dead tree's wood breaks down into soil, nurturing the growth of new seedlings.

Wondering how to design something? Go outside and take a look

You don't have to travel to some exotic place to see how nature works. Just go out to your backyard and look at how every organism has adapted so elegantly to even the smallest habitat. Often the technological solutions we need to live sustainably on the planet exist just outside our door. Biomimicry has already been used as the model for many products—polar bear feet have inspired running shoes; the burrs on plants led to Velcro. But how else is biomimicry changing scientific thought? Have a look!

High-performance silk:
Dr. David Knight and Dr. Fritz Vollrath (Oxford Biomaterials) devise novel ways to copy a spider's ability to spin silks without using heat or toxic chemicals. The new material, called Spidrex, is amazingly tough and may be used for medical sutures or protective clothing worn by rescue workers.

Super-tiny solar cell:
Dr. Devens Gust and Drs. Thomas and Ana Moore (Arizona State University) study how leaves capture energy so they can create artificial photosynthesis systems capable of producing and storing energy in tiny, sun-powered batteries.

Self-cleaning clothes: Dr. Wilhelm Barthlott (Nees Institute for Biodiversity of Plants) and his colleagues imitated the natural ability of lotus leaves to repel dirt by creating "smart surface" fabrics and paints that can virtually clean themselves. Touch water to the surface and it beads up, rolling the dirt away with it.

Underwater glue: Mussels attach themselves to rocks with an adhesive strong enough to withstand crashing waves. Dr. Russell Stewart (University of Utah) studies the chemical properties of the mussels' incredible sticky threads with the hopes of creating medical glues that can stick to wet surfaces inside human bodies.

Gecko-foot Band-Aids: Dr. Jeffrey Karp (Brigham and Women's Hospital) created bandages covered with millions of teeny-tiny pillars that mimic the nanoscopic (even tinier than microscopic) bristles—called setae—found on the bottom of geckos' feet. Setae use an intermolecular attraction to allow gecko feet to stick to almost any surface. These bandages could soon close wounds without stitches.

Natural cures: Dr. Sabrina Krief (National Museum of Natural History in Paris) and her colleagues watched chimps in Uganda eating certain leaves mixed with dirt each morning and discovered that the combination was effective in protecting them from malaria, a deadly disease that also affects humans.

MEET AN EXPERT!

Bryony Schwan
Biomimicry Institute, United States

Bryony grew up in Zimbabwe. Her parents often took her into the bush to watch African wildlife. She spent many years as an adult working on conservation issues such as deforestation and toxic chemicals. Eventually, she grew very tired of telling people what not to do. She wanted to inspire them with hopeful examples of what to do instead. Then her friend Janine Benyus wrote a book called *Biomimicry: Innovation Inspired by Nature* and launched the Biomimicry Institute. Bryony knew this was where she wanted to devote her work.

Bryony's advice for the decade ahead: Don't be put in a box

The further you go in school, the more specialized your studies become. If you decide to become an engineer, you tend to study only math and physics. Bryony believes kids should keep taking art and biology no matter what they think they might like to be when they grow up. So many universities now want to add biomimicry to their engineering and design schools, she and her colleagues at the Biomimicry Institute can't keep up with the demand. That's a good problem if we want to raise people who will think to ask, "How would nature do this?"

Mmmm...chocolate chip cookies. The smell of baking is wafting through the house, making your stomach growl.

But hang on a sec—does homemade mean homegrown? Just how far did those ingredients travel before they were mixed, scooped, and baked in your oven? As it turns out, even the humble homemade chocolate chip cookie has come a long way to reach your tummy.

About 9,000 years ago, humans began to make the transition away from hunting and gathering to keeping animals and planting seeds. Farming was born, and it changed how we feed ourselves. Unlike gray whales, which swim all the way from the birthing lagoons in Mexico to the Arctic—the equivalent of 320,000 lengths of an Olympic swimming pool—to find food, we expect food to travel to the stores where we buy it. It takes huge amounts of fossil fuels to grow, process, package, and transport many of the everyday foods we eat. We've become used to eating non-local and out-of-season food all year round. All of those bananas, oranges, and strawberries that you buy in middle of winter have to come from some place hot that's far, far away.

Which brings us to that chocolate chip cookie. Sure, it was baked at home, but it's quite likely that the vanilla used to make it came from Madagascar, the sugar from Brazil, and the chips from cacao beans grown in West Africa. That's quite a lot of travel, or food miles. One science journalist was curious to see just how much fuel was used to get him a meal. So he calculated the amount of oil it takes to get him a week's worth of breakfast of oatmeal, frozen organic raspberries, and a cup of fair-trade coffee. The result? Two liters (half a gallon)! Pour that in your car and your family could do a week's worth of local errands.

Whether it's breakfast, lunch, or dinner, each meal you eat typically includes ingredients from at least five countries. Where our food comes from and how it's grown and shipped is important to us and the other animal species we share the Earth with. That's because we use more than a third of the world's surface to plant our crops and graze the cattle and other animals we eat. That's amazing when you consider all of the cities combined cover just a tiny 3% of the land surface.

So here's the important thing: Everywhere, new ideas are popping up about how to feed you, me, and the rest of Earth's 6.8 billion people in ways the planet can sustain. The real challenge is pulling them together to produce enough food and a healthy, happy world. Sound impossible? *Let's have a look...*

THE BATTLE FOR YOUR BELLY

See that food on your plate? How did it get there? And what's the best way to grow it?

Ask a question about your food and you're as likely to hear from an economist or a scientist as a farmer in coveralls who plows a field. That's because much of the world's farming is done by industrial agriculture. It uses science and mechanical know-how to grow more food more cheaply on less land. But many people are worried about how industrial agriculture's methods affect the planet and our health. They prefer natural, organic farming methods. It's set up one BIG battle over how we get our food: Who do you support?

Captain Industrial Agriculture

Who is the captain?

Responsible for most of your grocery store's food, the captain's super-sized farms specialize in just one or a few crops. Petroleum-based fertilizers and pesticides protect his crops from insects and help them grow quickly. In the laboratory, the captain creates genetically modified (GM) crops to supply ingredients for more than half the items sold in supermarkets in North America— everything from bread to tomatoes, breakfast cereal to salad dressing.

Does he help us?

By growing more food cheaply on less land, industrial agriculture saves more natural areas from being cleared for farming. Many believe it is the only way to produce enough food to feed the rapidly increasing number of people on the planet.

Or does he hurt us?

Not everyone loves the captain. Those in favor of sustainable agriculture say he uses tons of fossil fuels that are running out and can't be replaced. He also gulps so much water that once-fertile areas become deserts. His pesticides and fertilizers can pollute the water, killing frogs, birds, fish, and other animals.

Heroes or villains? If only it was so easy!

The challenge of growing food, of course, is that many issues are complicated. New maps show that the Earth is rapidly running out of fertile farmland. At the same time, the world's population is growing, growing, growing! Is Captain Industrial Agriculture a hero because he can produce high yields of food? Or is he a villain because he uses

vs. Super Sustainable Farmers

Meet the new farmers

New ways to farm that are better for soil, water, air, and other species are emerging everywhere. Biodiversity ranchers, for example, rotate their cattle through grasslands on schedules that maximize their beef production and protect fragile wild plants and animals. Compare a satellite image of the Sahel region of Niger, Africa, with one taken thirty years ago and you'll see that it's far greener today. Millions of trees now thrive thanks to poor farmers who nurtured the saplings, carefully plowing around them when sowing peanuts, beans, and millet. Farmers now eat the fruits and feed the seed pods to their livestock. They cut branches from the living trees and sell them for money. The roots hold the water in the ground rather than letting it flood villages and destroy crops. The trees supply life for the eighty-five species of migratory birds that pass over your house on their way to feed in Niger each winter. A green oasis flourishes where a desert once spread.

Is everyone fed?

Captain Industrial Agriculture claims that organic and other sustainable farming approaches may work fine in small doses, but they could never supply enough food to feed the world. Super Sustainable Farmers say that by growing lots of kinds of food that are appropriate to each location on farms of many sizes, they can supply enough food while keeping the water and soil ecosystems that we all need nourished.

so much petroleum-based chemicals and water to do so? The real question isn't whether it's good or bad. Instead, we need to creatively combine different styles of farming to produce enough food while reducing our need for fossil fuels, improving water and soil quality, and preserving wildlife and wild places.

DECODER

It's the eco-farming decoder sheet!

There are a lot of terms thrown around when people talk about farming today, but what do they actually mean? Let's check them out quick!

Organic: Food produced this way follows a simple principle—animals nourish the soil that nourishes the plants. Organic farming prohibits the use of synthetic (human-made) chemicals, though it can use chemicals from plants, minerals, or other natural sources.

Local food: This is food grown or produced within your community or region—usually within 160 km (100 miles) of your home.

Biodiversity: This refers to the diversity of species and habitats in a particular place. The Amazon rainforest, for instance, has a very high natural biodiversity because hundreds of thousands of different species of plants and animals live there. Planting hedgerows where birds and insects can thrive along the edges of farm fields is an example of biodiversity farming.

Sustainable agriculture: This seeks to produce crops in ways that won't destroy the environment, health, or livelihood of current or future generations. Producing high yields today in a way that leads to drought, soil erosion, and poor crops in twenty years' time is unsustainable.

Yield: The amount of crop harvested per unit (such as an acre or bushel) over a given time.

FARMING FOR THE CITY

Wouldn't it be great if big cities could grow their own food? It's not as crazy an idea as it seems!

Okay, so you know that growing some of your own food will reduce food miles. But what if you, like more than half the people on Earth, live in a crowded city? No worries. Urban farming is a hot new trend, and it's sprouting up in surprising places. Vacant lots and concrete balconies burst with tomatoes, peas, squash, and other vegetables. Unused railway tracks and people's yards blossom with apples, peaches, and plums. Friendly guerrilla gardeners in London, England, get together each year to harvest the lavender they plant on traffic islands in the city. Everywhere places are being turned into urban gardens.

The original vertical farmers

Vertical farming has been going on in the wild for millions of years. Orangutans move slowly through the tropical rainforests of Southeast Asia. As they feast, they poop, spreading the seeds of the next generation of trees.

Squash on floor fourteen

The biggest challenge to farming in a city is finding enough open space to do it. Cities have the same problem with homes—that's why they build tall skyscrapers where hundreds of people can live on a fairly small area of land. Now engineers are trying to do the same thing with farming—that's right, vertical skyscraper farms may soon be providing year-round crops to a city near you. By going up rather than sprawling out, vertical farms take up much less land than traditional farms. Scientists have designed prototypes for a farm building thirty stories tall and the size of a New York City block that could grow enough food to feed 50,000 people a year!

Tomatoes on the roof, peas on the wall

Why stop with the ground when you can grow things on buildings, too? Students and volunteers grow vegetables on a campus rooftop at McGill University in Montreal and harvest the produce for a local meals-on-wheels program. Take a balloon ride over Vancouver's new convention center and you'll discover a meadow of native plants buzzing with bees. Green roofs covered with soil and plants are becoming quite common in many European countries, such as Germany, Switzerland, and the Netherlands. Even a wall of Madrid's Caixa Forum museum is alive with around 15,000 plants of 250 different species.

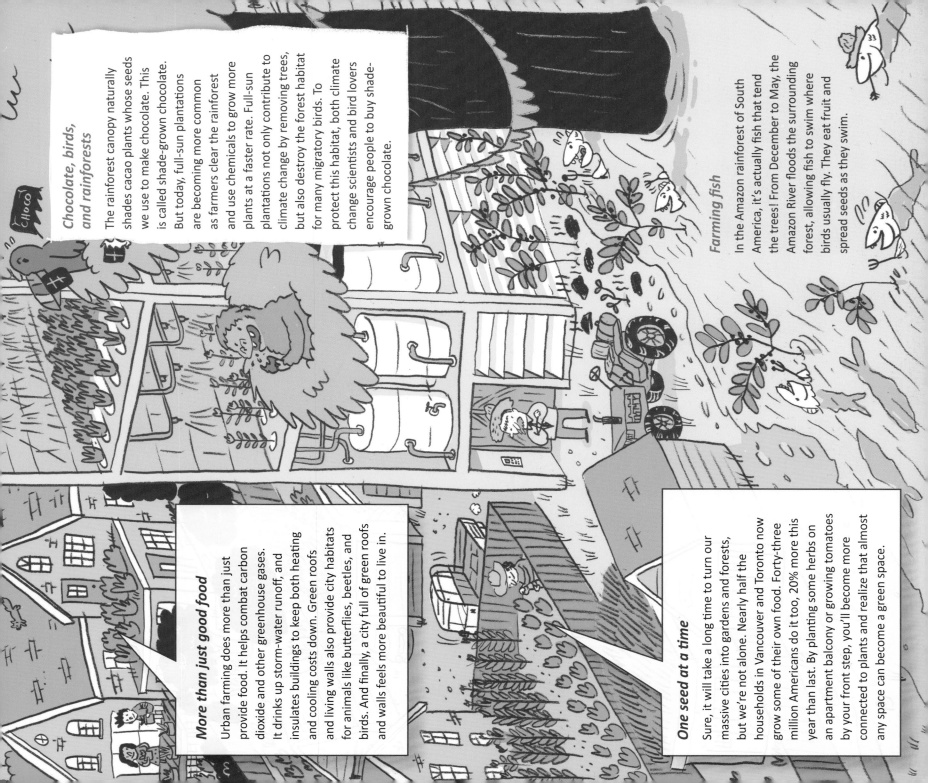

Chocolate, birds, and rainforests

The rainforest canopy naturally shades cacao plants whose seeds we use to make chocolate. This is called shade-grown chocolate. But today, full-sun plantations are becoming more common as farmers clear the rainforest and use chemicals to grow more plants at a faster rate. Full-sun plantations not only contribute to climate change by removing trees, but also destroy the forest habitat for many migratory birds. To protect this habitat, both climate change scientists and bird lovers encourage people to buy shade-grown chocolate.

Farming fish

In the Amazon rainforest of South America, it's actually fish that tend the trees! From December to May, the Amazon River floods the surrounding forest, allowing fish to swim where birds usually fly. They eat fruit and spread seeds as they swim.

More than just good food

Urban farming does more than just provide food. It helps combat carbon dioxide and other greenhouse gases. It drinks up storm-water runoff, and insulates buildings to keep both heating and cooling costs down. Green roofs and living walls also provide city habitats for animals like butterflies, beetles, and birds. And finally, a city full of green roofs and walls feels more beautiful to live in.

One seed at a time

Sure, it will take a long time to turn our massive cities into gardens and forests, but we're not alone. Nearly half the households in Vancouver and Toronto now grow some of their own food. Forty-three million Americans do it too, 20% more this year than last. By planting some herbs on an apartment balcony or growing tomatoes by your front step, you'll become more connected to plants and realize that almost any space can become a green space.

MEET A LOCAL FOODS CHEF

Luke Hayes-Alexander

**Luke's Gastronomy restaurant,
Kingston, Ontario, Canada**

How one boy turned his love of local food into a unique restaurant

Luke was born in 1990 and grew up in his parents' restaurant. When he was eleven years old, he decided to teach himself to become a chef and to dedicate himself to foods that are grown or raised locally. His dad and mom helped by teaching him everything they knew. He did lots of experimenting in the kitchen. He read about cooking and created journals filled with recipes he invented. Finally, when he was fifteen, Luke became the executive chef of Luke's Gastronomy.

Local food in the middle of the winter?

Kingston is close to Ottawa, the capital of Canada, and one of the coldest capital cities in the world! Luke admits that in the middle of winter, it can grate on your nerves when you see a cookbook full of tropical fruits and all you have available are roots and apples. But committing to local foods makes him a more creative chef. When preparing winter parsnips, he draws upon a Roman recipe from hundreds of years ago. Hints of spice, hints of herbs, some cheese, and then honey and white wine—everything together creates a delicious complexity of tastes. Even parsnips can taste great!

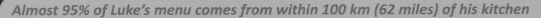

Almost 95% of Luke's menu comes from within 100 km (62 miles) of his kitchen

At first it felt like a chore to do all the research necessary to find local sources for ingredients. Now that Luke has a great network of farmers and suppliers to draw from, it's easy. Mornings begin with shopping and going to the local market—one of the oldest in Canada—where food is delivered from thirty small farms in the area. Then it's back to the restaurant to prepare food for the day. When the restaurant opens, Luke is plating the food he has prepared based on what the customers order. When the doors close, it's time to clean up for the following day.

Global tastes, local flavors

Many of Luke's inspirations come from history or from other cultures around the world. He loves doing all of the research to discover what was popular to eat a thousand years ago. His favorite thing is to combine very old, time-honored, and traditional tastes with new and avant-garde flavors. Two time eras, one plate. In particular, Luke adores the wild fennel salami he makes in the traditional Tuscan style.

Cooking for happiness

No matter how interesting the food or how ancient the recipe, the number one thing Luke thinks about is creating meals that make people happy. When people are sitting down in a very nice atmosphere, getting wonderful service from his mom out front, and they're eating food that they find to be completely delicious, it fills him with joy. He is as happy cooking the food as they are eating it.

Luke's tips for eating locally

1. Shop at local farmers' markets.

2. Order local foods online. Believe it or not, many small farmers have good websites you can order from.

3. Find a company that sources food from many local farms and delivers it to your doorstep.

4. Look at the labels in your supermarket to find foods grown closer to your home.

In the decade ahead

Eating local foods is becoming very popular. Luke believes it will become an ordinary part of our everyday lives. That's good news, he says, because eating locally encourages more people to keep farming and it helps each of us to see food as a connection to our own communities. Plus, he's found that local foods taste better and have a better texture because they haven't been jostled about during lengthy transport and we're more likely to eat them when they are in season. Bite into a ripe, juicy peach at the height of summer from a local farmers' market to taste the difference.

THE REAL VALUE OF NATURE

Ever wondered how much a forest—and all of things it does for us and our environment—is actually worth? That's one of the big questions ecological economics helps us answer.

Eco-log-i-cal eco-no-mics (noun)

The way a country manages its money and resources (such as workers and land) to produce, buy, and sell goods and services within the natural limits of the Earth.

For sale: One planet

Imagine you are an all-powerful being holding a garage sale for the universe—what price tag would you place on nature? Or pretend that a rainforest works for your company. What would you pay it for all the jobs it does for the planet? A team of ecological economists previously calculated the value of all the services nature provides Earth—this includes stuff like clean water, clean air, fertile soils, and so forth. They came up with a whopping value of $33 trillion a year. If you spent $1 million every day, it would take you more than 9,000 years to reach that amount.

The bug bidding starts at $57 billion

They're so tiny we rarely give them a second thought—except to swat them away. But if we had to pay insects for all that they do for us, it would cost a fortune too. A team of ecological economists recently tabulated the minimum value of the free labor insects deliver in the United States alone. Insects are food for wildlife that supports a $50-billion recreation industry. Native insects provide more than $4.5 billion in pest control, pollinate $3 billion in crops, and clean up grazing lands with a subsequent savings to ranchers of more than $380 million. Without bugs to put food on our tables and decompose our waste, humans—and most other life on Earth—couldn't exist. Thanks, you hard-working bugs!

Now that's a capital idea

Economists call anything with some value *capital*. Bikes, shoes, houses, and other human-made things are called *physical capital*. *Financial capital* is the fancy name given to actual money, whether it's dollars or pesos or euros. *Human capital* refers to assets such as knowledge and skills and good health. A country that has a lot of doctors and teachers, for example, is rich in human capital.

Ecological economists pay close attention to *natural capital*. Figuring out the cost of wood or fish to buy or sell isn't too difficult. The trickier challenge is to estimate the value of the things the Earth does to support life. For example, the water from your faucet may have been purified by a wetland or perhaps the root system of an entire forest. Or how much pest control would a protected piece of land supply to the people living around it? Ecological economists create software systems and GIS (geographical information system) maps that make it easy for planners to answer those sorts of questions.

Money talks!

So why come up with these figures anyway? Ecological economists found the total economic value of a forest is at least three times more than the value of its wood for burning and building! These experts say the best way to conserve nature is to prove that it's worth a lot—alive.

MEET AN EXPERT!
Dr. Gretchen Daily
Stanford University, United States

Gretchen grew up partly in California and always loved the outdoors. Her family moved to Europe at a time when people were very concerned about pollution. She lived in Germany, where forests and lakes were highly valued and yet were becoming acidified. Inspired by people using huge social movements to demand solutions for environmental problems, she became an ecological economist.

Gretchen's forecast for the next decade

Today, most investors appraise the worth of land simply by figuring out what might be built on it, mined from it, or farmed on it. Gretchen believes that in the decade ahead, planners will use new tools to help them recognize and make decisions based on the economic value of nature.

What would you pack to live on the moon?

An ice cream maker? A flashlight? Your dog? Gretchen likes to challenge people with this question because it shows how totally we depend on Earth. Our planet gives us food, drink, shelter, clothing, and fun. It supplies basic life support, such as a stable climate and pure water. None of us could survive without the natural capital we get free from Earth.

TALES FROM YOUR LUNCHBOX!

From seaweed in your ice cream to bugs in your... well, everything. You'd be surprised by what you'll eat!

You usually think of food as coming from things like fruits and vegetables or chickens that were raised to be eaten. But many of your favorite tastes are unexpectedly connected to wild plants and animals that live on land and in the ocean.

Raise a toast to the ocean if you like ice cream

Seaweed, algae, and microscopic ocean plants produce about half of the world's oxygen. And certain types of seaweed are a big part of Asian diets and used in meals like sushi. But can you guess what puts the creamy texture into ice cream and toothpaste, makes margarine thick, and even prevents the paint on your bedroom wall from smearing? It's one of the fastest-growing plants on Earth—kelp. This enormous algae can grow as long as your arm in a day. It's even nicknamed the Cinderella plant because of its diverse and helpful qualities.

It may not say "seaweed" on the label, but...

Kelp is a perfect example of how certain plants that you'd probably never see as being yummy are a big part of some of your favorite treats. Next time you're in the shop count the number of times you see seaweed ingredients such as algin or carrageenan in your brand of salad dressing, jelly, sauces, soap, creamy candy, cosmetics, and medicines. Neat, huh? Even if you're not eating them, aquatic plants can help your food in other ways, too. Kelp has teeny-tiny cousins that are single-celled algae called diatoms. Diatoms have extremely intricate bodies composed of silica glass. Apple juice producers create the clear liquid you love to drink by pouring naturally cloudy juices through filters made from the glass skeletons of these microscopic floating jewels of the sea.

Speaking of food...

Okay, so we got you to admit that you like eating seaweed. Now how about bugs? If you were playing soccer with a group of friends in central Africa, you might stop for a quick snack of ants or grubs rather than raisins or cookies. After a concert in Southeast Asia, you'd flock to a street vendor to buy fried crickets. In over one hundred countries people enjoy entomophagy (en-toh-MOFF-uh-jee), the fine art of eating bugs. Lately, insects have been found on the menus of some of the trendiest restaurants in North America and Europe.

You're already eating some insects anyway

As it turns out, eating insects is a great way to reduce your ecological footprint (for more on that, see page 46). They are super low fat, high in minerals and protein, and much easier, cleaner, and more efficient to raise than beef or pork. Still not convinced? Sorry, but it's actually impossible to remove insects entirely from the foods we eat. Government agencies have created guidelines for the number of bug parts allowable in retail foods. Chocolate can have sixty insect fragments per 100 grams (3.5 oz), and 225 parts are allowed in a box of macaroni and cheese. Each year, we each eat about a kilo (2.2 pounds) of insect fragments. But don't sweat it—according to nutritionists, we're all the healthier for it.

Even more reasons to be grateful to bugs (and fish, too)

Here's a riddle for you—how do pond-dwelling fish that you'd never dream of eating still manage to get food on your plate? Glad you asked! Adult dragonflies are big eaters of bees, butterflies, and other insect pollinators. However, fish in ponds eat dragonfly larvae. Nurture a pond and fish will thrive. The result is an unexpected cascade: The more fish, the fewer dragonflies, the more bees, the more plant pollination, and ultimately, the more food—for you!

The tiny heroes of chocolate lovers

No one shouts "Hurray" when midges start biting your flesh at the beach. As you scratch those bites, you might not be impressed that midges have the fastest wing beat of any creature on Earth (1,000 beats a second!), or that they're so small that they fit easily on the head of a pin. But did you know that midges are the only known pollinators of cultivated cacao—that's the plant whose beans your chocolate chips were made from. Hurray!

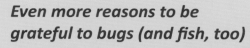

Careful where you step

The next time you're playing on a field, take a moment to consider all the beasts that live there. On average, 10,000 insects live in every sidewalk-square-sized portion of habitable land on Earth. Strict followers of Jainism, one of the world's oldest religions, believe in *ahimsa* (the avoidance of harm). They have tiny points on the bottom of their shoes to reduce the possibility of accidentally stepping on all those precious insects.

HOW BEES ARE CONNECTED TO YOUR BURGER AND WORLD PEACE

What kind of super insect fills your tummy and could make war zones safer?

You won't bee-lieve the answer!

Thousands of years ago: Ancestors of modern honeybees originally lived in Africa. Thanks to people moving them around through history, you'll see them nearly everywhere on Earth these days...

Today: ...including in your favorite park, ruining your nice picnic. Hey!

But hang on a sec. Without these winged wonders, the chocolate in those chocolate chip cookies and most of your picnic would vanish. No kidding.

Heya!

pollen

Bees are pollinators. They carry a flower's male pollen to the female parts of other flowers. Without pollination, new flowering plants could not grow.

One out of every three bites of food you consume depends on the amazing pollinating power of bees—and that can even include meat, too!

The diet of cattle and many other animals includes alfalfa, clover, and other forage crops that bees pollinate.

Plus some bees also make honey, which humans (and bears) love!

But bees do more than tend the garden. A few lucky ones are training to be peacekeepers, too!

In countries recovering from war, like Croatia, scientists have trained bees to use their amazing sense of smell to find explosives, bombs, and landmines that are preventing people from farming again.

A few years ago: Beekeepers across the United States, Canada, Australia, China, Brazil, and Europe report that millions of worker bees simply disappeared. Vibrant colonies become bee ghost towns.

What is killing the bees?
It's a mystery looking for an answer.

Some researchers feel that mite parasites have grown resistant to pesticides and are infesting bees, making bees more likely to get sick from viruses or bacteria.

Other scientists think certain chemicals used to grow food or green lawns harm the bees' memories—they can't find their way back to their hives and get lost.

Help out by planting bee-friendly gardens and leaving dead tree stumps where bees build hives. Find a list of local plants that bees love online or at a nursery.

The bees you help today will keep food on your table. Live on, you striped superheroes!

WHAT'S THE MOST PRECIOUS LIQUID IN THE ENTIRE UNIVERSE?

Water!

Tweet! The referee blows the whistle and you stagger off the field in search of a BIG drink. Water, juice, sports drinks… you'd drink yak milk if that was the only choice. Your body needs about two liters (half a gallon) of water daily. You couldn't survive more than three days without it. But the vast amount of the water we humans use isn't what we drink or even bathe in. It's the incredible amount used by industrial agriculture to grow our food. It takes at least 2,000 liters (528 gallons) to produce just one day of food for each of us. In fact, irrigation is such a thirsty business, it uses more than 70% of all the fresh water drawn on Earth for human use. Many people say it's time that we learn to grow food in ways that conserve water. After all, water is the most precious liquid in the universe.

Follow the water

That's what astronomers (scientists who study outer space) do as they search the universe for signs of life. Water is actually found everywhere, from vast interstellar dust clouds to the orange-red fields of Mars. But most of it exists as ice, which can't support life. With the help of Herschel, the largest imaging space telescope, Canadian and European scientists are probing different space environments for liquid water.

In the name of safer, cleaner water

It's difficult to imagine that people could go thirsty on a planet that is so rich in water. Yet nearly one billion people struggle to find safe water to drink. Children and women in poorer countries travel an average of 6 km (4 miles) every day to collect water, and even then it may not be clean enough to drink. International agencies, like the United Nations Children's Fund (UNICEF), work in countries all over the world to try to change this. So how would you bring water to people in need? Here are some ideas to inspire you.

- *Water filter in a cup:* A group of artists called Potters for Peace and scientists at the Massachusetts Institute of Technology (MIT) are working on inexpensive ceramic filters that fit in a cup and clean the water as you drink.

- *Water filter in a straw:* The Lifestraw allows people to safely drink from a muddy puddle or unknown water source.

- *You spin, it pumps:* PlayPumps use specially designed roundabouts to pump clean drinking water to a community well whenever kids play.

- *By the time you get back home...:* Aquaduct is a prototype adult-sized tricycle with a large water tank in back. Pedaling draws water through a filter to another removable tank up front.

- *And finally...:* Sign on to a United Nations international agreement that states that every person on Earth has the right to clean water.

Feeling thirsty? Head for the tap

Meanwhile, back on planet Earth it's easy to see why they call Canada a water-rich nation. Only Brazil and Russia have more renewable fresh water. Yet instead of turning on the tap, Canadians consume more than 2 billion bottles of water a year. In the United States—which has its own rich sources of fresh water—people consume more bottled water than beer, coffee, and milk combined. How do they get all of that bottled water?

Factories burn 18 million barrels of oil and consume 41 billion gallons of fresh water every day—just to make bottled water that most people in North America don't need. That's why a growing number of cities, such as New York, San Francisco, and Paris, are pulling the plug on bottled water. Instead, they're promoting tap water as the safe and healthy alternative to expensive and environmentally unfriendly bottled water.

Chapter Three

TECHNO PLANET
It's a cyber revolution!

Beep! Boing! Whirr! Is that your phone or is someone playing a video game on a laptop?

Computer sounds are such an ordinary part of your life, you may not even realize how new they are to the planet. You're one of the first generations in history to have known personal computers your whole lives. Thanks to GPS (global positioning system) technology, you're also the first generation of people who may never know what it feels like to get lost. And you're the first generation to play in virtual worlds so real, you may feel more at home in a SIMS video game than in the park around the corner!

The thing about this cyber revolution is that it's happening fast! With computers doubling in speed roughly every two years, and newer sleeker, models surging onto the market, it's easy to keep on buying. But all that new stuff comes with a big environmental price tag. Every day, people in the United States throw out 130,000 computers and twice as many cell phones. Technology spits out this new type of deadly trash—e-waste—so quickly, it's created a whole new trade in international garbage.

It's against the law in many places, but e-waste is often shipped to and dumped in poorer countries where environmental regulations are not as strict. People who have the least opportunity to buy expensive computers end up dealing with the deadly waste those computers produce. Yet there's a surprising connection—YouTube, online news, and other computer-based media make it easier to expose these kinds of problems to the world...and to create action to fix them!

All that technology also means that you can connect with animals around the planet in ways like never before. Over 3 million web users, for instance, logged on to watch eleven endangered leatherback sea turtles race 6,000 km (3,700 miles) from the frigid waters of Canada, where they feed, to the nesting beaches of the Caribbean. Seeing the world through the eyes of a sea turtle was so touching, that many of these people started helping to protect them.

From satellite tags on the fins of whales to chips on the wings of butterflies, cell phones, digital recorders, and other computer technologies log incredible details of wild lives. Want to see? *Just turn the page...*

THE OCEAN ON SPEED DIAL

The same technologies that tempt you indoors reveal amazing new facts about life in the wild.

Whales, sharks, tuna, elephant seals…while you are reading this, hundreds of open-ocean animals are beaming messages up to satellites. Tiny electronic satellite tags fixed to their fins and flippers capture information about water temperature, depth, and the animals' location. Researchers in labs and coffee shops all over the world download the data onto their cell phones or laptops and use it to create richer computer models of how oceans—and ocean animals—function.

Now that's a marathon swimmer!

Scientists are discovering that many ocean-going animals migrate much farther distances than ever imagined. Trevor, a Pacific bluefin tuna, crossed the Pacific Ocean three times in just twenty months—a distance greater than swimming around the world. Bluefin tuna are warm-blooded giants. They can grow as long as a canoe and as heavy as the combined weight of all the kids in your class. But what these fish are really famous for is their speed. They clock speeds as fast as cars on a highway—100 kph (60 mph)—when chasing down a tasty meal of anchovies, herring, eels, or squid.

And an astronomer, too!

A great white shark named Nicole swam from South Africa to Australia and back—a round-trip journey of almost 20,000 km (12,500 miles). Although she frequently dove to depths of a kilometer (half a mile) or more, Nicole mostly swam along the surface. This fact led researchers to suspect that great white sharks may navigate using the stars. (Hey, I've got water in my eyes. Is that the North Star?)

Tuna on the turnpike, sharks on the freeway

What's exciting about these new findings is not just how incredibly far or fast some species swim, but also how predictable their routes are. It's as if they are traveling on marine highways that are invisible to human eyes. Knowing where ocean animals travel is vital for conservation. Ships steaming into Boston, Massachusetts, for example, must now shift 6 km (4 miles) north of their old path to prevent collisions with endangered whales in the first whale feeding sanctuary in the United States.

Ocean traffic

Technology enables us to understand life in the ocean in ways we never could with just our eyes. Spot a humpback whale off the coast of Norway, for instance, and it's likely to be alone. But by using the navy's anti-submarine listening stations, whale researchers are able to track the locations of whales using computer images of their voices. The images reveal that these "solitary" whales are actually traveling together at distances as far as 50 km (30 miles) apart! It turns out that whales have incredible hearing and they keep in touch through sound. Blue whales, for instance, can communicate across an ocean just by using sound.

Sadly, whales, tuna, and other ocean animals are being bombarded by the collective noise of boats. Tanker ships are incredibly noisy beasts. Drop a hydrophone (underwater microphone) into a busy shipping lane and the sound is as loud as the middle of an expressway. And the amount of ship traffic is increasing each year. There's a good chance that the computer in your home or school was manufactured in and shipped from China. It will likely be shipped back to China when you're through with it. Altogether, shipping goods adds up to a whopping 100 million container loads crisscrossing the world's oceans each year. Using technology, researchers can pinpoint how sensitive whale hearing is. They can show how rapidly the ocean is becoming a noisier place. This makes them better able to argue for restrictions on shipping routes and new technologies to make boats quieter.

Whales that don't migrate?

Fin whales are the second-largest animals on Earth. And they're fast. Nicknamed the "greyhounds of the sea," these giants travel the same speed as cars in a school zone. Like most large baleen whales, they migrate, swimming to the poles each summer to gorge in the cold, food-rich waters. Yet recently scientists discovered something quite unusual—400 fin whales living in the Gulf of California, Mexico, that don't migrate. The gulf may turn out to be one of the only places on Earth capable of producing enough food to support these giants all year round. That's a great clue that it's a super-special place worth protecting.

And bushes that do?!

Video games rely on huge databases of information to create the imaginary worlds in which you play. Scientists use similarly huge databases of information about species and habitats to explore changes on our planet over time. A study of French mountain forests reveals that climate change is driving hundreds of plant species up hillsides. Wait, walking bushes? Are they crazy? The forest ecosystem, not just individual plants, has moved more than 18.5 m (60 feet) higher since you were born. While the short-lived bushes and grasses take root higher and higher in search of ideal temperature conditions, the long-lived trees are left behind, making it harder for us to notice how quickly things are changing.

THINK FASTER! THINK LONGER!

What will your great-great-great-great-great-grandchildren like to play?

Zwap! Your lightning-fast fingers save the virtual world from invading aliens on your game console. Thanks to higher-speed upgrades, you can react to a lightsaber duel in a flash. Video games and web searches train you to expect results in milliseconds. But practicing how to think in really long time scales is important, too. Indigenous peoples call this "seven-generational thinking"—the act of considering the impact of our decisions on people who will live on Earth seven generations from now.

The dark side of clean technology

Future thinking is essential with e-waste. That's because the 20 to 50 million tonnes (22 to 55 million tons) of dead consoles, televisions, monitors, and other e-waste tossed out each year contains lead, cadmium, mercury, and other toxic chemicals. You don't have to worry about them when they're safely doing their jobs inside your computer or MP3 player, but if they get loose in the dump—watch out! They're more evil than Darth Vader and they'll stick around long enough to affect the health of your great-great-great-great-great (and even your not so great!) grandchildren. So instead of dumping the gaming console you got on your last birthday (yep, that old dinosaur), google one of these cool e-cyclers. Depending on the site, they'll buy new, used, or broken electronics in exchange for cash, store credit, or a charitable donation!

Best Buy • Earth911 • Gazelle • NextWorth
BuyMyTronics • Amazon Video Game Trade-In

Welcome to 2051

©2008

Want a job in computers? Focus on e-waste

The European Union, or EU (that's what e-waste is: "Eeew!"), recently passed strict regulations placing all companies that make electronics responsible for collecting their old products and recycling them. The companies are not allowed to ship this e-waste off to other countries with lower health and environmental standards. And non-EU countries feel growing pressure to do the same thing. What does this mean for your future? For one thing, they'll be many new careers in "Green IT" (information technology). You could discover new materials that would make computers less toxic in the first place. Or design more efficient systems for turning old computers back into new ones. Whether you're keen on working with international law, how video games are designed and marketed, or how computers could be powered by the sun, there's a host of green-collar jobs waiting for you.

Your cell phone will pop in 2...1...0 seconds!

Screws lose their threads and thrust themselves out. Hooks straighten and push other pieces away. Glues melt. Plastics dissolve into powder. Welcome to the world of design for disassembly—designing things to break apart on purpose. In the race to design better recyclable electronics, the faster something comes apart, the quicker it can be recycled and the less energy and money it demands. Nokia, a cell phone company, designed a prototype cell phone that snaps itself apart in two seconds. The whole thing is heat-triggered. Just point a laser beam and POP!

E-waste–munching microbes to the rescue

Bacteria may be tiny, but they could be heroes in the battle to dispose of e-waste. Some leach, or remove, lead, copper, and tin from printed circuit boards. Others can separate aluminum, copper, nickel, zinc, and gold from e-waste dust. Many people believe the potential for bio-leaching bacteria to safely recover precious metals from toxic dust is giant. This promises a much cleaner way to reach the valuable metals inside than the dangerous but common practice of melting down old monitors and other electronics.

Elin Explains

HOW VIDEO GAMES AND CELL PHONES ARE CONNECTED TO GORILLAS

Can your electronic toys and gadgets really affect jungles in Africa? *Find out how!*

Millions of people around the world play video games and talk on cell phones.

These video game consoles—as well as popular devices like MP3 players and computers—are made using a rare mineral called coltan.

High demand for coltan creates a modern-day gold rush around the world. Everyone wants more coltan!

In Africa: One of the world's important sources of coltan exists in Kahuzi-Biega National Park in the Democratic Republic of Congo.

The park is also home to many animals that live in its rainforests, including rare mountain gorillas and eastern lowland gorillas.

As the price for coltan goes up, illegal miners flood into the park, making it unsafe for the gorillas.

Rebel leaders also fight over control of the area. They even force poor men, women, and children into illegal mining for coltan.

Wildlife and human rights organizations demand that computer companies buy coltan only from legal mines that treat people and wildlife fairly.

Meanwhile: Millions of dollars of coltan and other precious metals are lost every year in thrown-out computers and cell phones.

2008: 1.2 billion cell phones are sold. Only 1% are recycled—that's a lot of wasted coltan. More recycling will mean less harmful mining!

Europe: It's becoming the law! Companies must take back used electronics and recycle or dispose of them in ecologically friendly ways, so...

...many companies start to design to disassemble! They design products that are easier to take apart so they can be recycled.

North America: Kids launch school campaigns to recycle old cell phones and trade video games with friends instead of buying new ones.

Elsewhere in Africa: Dr. Emma Stokes brings hope for apes everywhere. She finds evidence of 125,000 western lowland gorillas living in an unexplored area—if further studies confirm the numbers, it doubles their estimated population!

Recycling your video games and cell phones helps control the demand for coltan—and helps protect the future of gorillas in Africa!

NEW IMAGES OF AN OLD PLANET

Computers, satellites, and digital imaging revolutionize the way we map our world.

Since the beginning of history, people drew maps to understand the world and their place in it. If you lived before the 4th century BCE, you'd have drawn the Earth as flat. The Greek philosopher Aristotle drew maps with Earth as the center of the universe. Christopher Columbus, the famous explorer, mistakenly landed in South America rather than India because he relied on maps that showed the Earth to be much smaller than it actually is.

Find an old map of your neighborhood and you can peel back its history. In Vancouver, for example, fifty salmon-spawning streams exist on early maps of city blocks now covered with houses and schools. (Is that a fish in your locker?) We rely on current and reliable maps to shape the way we understand our places on the planet.

These days, you can see the world at a level of detail and accuracy even your parents couldn't have imagined when they were your age. Log onto Google Earth and you can virtually fly anywhere on the planet. Thinking of taking a trip to the tropics? Click on the satellite image and you can examine the rainforest canopy or even see the hotel where you plan to stay. GPS units equipped with mapping technologies speak to you from the dashboards of cars and guide you to restaurants or your aunt's apartment in an unfamiliar town.

Is this map really upside down?

By mapping where ocean animals congregate, we stop thinking of oceans as big bathtubs full of water and start seeing them as different habitats where certain animals are found and others are not, just as we see on land. How we map our own human world helps us to shift our understanding of life on Earth, too. Take this "south up" map, for example. Stuart McArthur of Melbourne, Australia, first drew it when he was twelve years old. He produced the first official "south up" version nine years later. Stuart's map reminds us that north doesn't have to be at the top. People started drawing maps that way when European explorers began using the North Star and the magnetic compass (which points north) to guide their ships. Before that, the top of the map was to the East, in what was then called the Orient. That's where the word "orientation" comes from, meaning knowing where you are positioned in relation to other things.

Tagged animals guide us to hidden treasures

Remember those electronic tags on the sharks and tuna? Data from remote-sensing devices enables scientists to map the oceans in extraordinary new ways. In recent years, teams of researchers have tagged more than 2,000 individual animals representing twenty-two different species of top predators—including whales, sea turtles, elephant seals, and seabirds that roam the Pacific Ocean. By combining the data collected from each individual, they've discovered biodiversity hot spots in the open ocean. Like watering holes in the African savanna, these hot spots are places where many species come together. Their presence supports entire, complex food webs of life. But unlike watering holes on land, the biodiversity hot spots in the oceans change location.

The dome is home

The Costa Rica Dome is an example of one of these moving hot spots. It is an area of water in the Pacific Ocean about 800 to 1,300 km (500 to 800 miles) west of Costa Rica. It's hard to find because its location changes depending on winds, water temperatures, and currents. Researchers were able to find it—and to recognize how important it is to protect—by using computer technology to follow individual animals to its location. And what they have found is amazing. By tracking blue whales to the Costa Rica Dome, researchers discovered a secret place where blue whales (the largest and among the most endangered animals on Earth) give birth to their gigantic babies.

Scaling up the view

Maps enable you to the see the world at a bigger scale than you can experience simply by walking around and looking at things. That ability to see beyond what your eyes can show you is particularly valuable now, at a time when what you and I and everyone else does has such a big collective impact. Obviously buying one video game is no big deal to the planet. But the $21 billion worth of video games sold just last year is. Curious about how big a deal? *Flip the page.*

PUT YOUR FOOT DOWN

> ### Eco·log·i·cal foot·prints (noun)
> *A measure of how much ecological capacity the Earth has and how much we use.*

Psssst...Hey, buddy, can you spare me a planet?

Thanks to the ability of computers to synthesize incredible amounts of data, you can access the information you need to draw maps of where rainforests are found on Earth. Or how many people borrow library books. Or how many video games an average child living in each country has. Whatever map you choose to draw, it will soon become obvious that some parts of the world use much more water, food, energy, and stuff than other places.

It's a really tough concept to grasp, but people living in places like North America use up so many resources that if everyone lived like that, we'd need more than just planet Earth to support us. How much more? FIVE EARTHS! And even if we squeezed down to the size of an average European lifestyle, we'd still need three Earths! Clearly that's impossible.

Now if we're using more than one planet's worth of resources, that means that other people—and other animals—are getting far less than their share. We've been borrowing resources from the people and other species who will live on the planet in the near future. For instance, humans are cutting down rainforests faster than they can re-grow. That means that we're leaving future generations an ecological debt in the form of deforestation, soil loss, extinction of species, and the accumulation of CO_2 in the atmosphere. Now that's not using seven-generational thinking!

Dr. Mathis Wackernagel (see the next page) and Dr. William Rees created a resource accounting tool called the ecological footprint. It helps countries keep track of how many resources they have and how much they are using. It's like a budget that highlights where we're overspending—by city, country, or the planet. The goal is to create new ways to live well within the ecological constraints of planet Earth. Call it one-planet living—not five!

We can live sustainably

You might think that keeping track of how fast humans are using up the planet's resources would be a depressing job, but Mathis doesn't see it that way. He believes that we can succeed in living sustainably, and that we have the business tools to do it. Here are the big questions to ask:

- How many resources do we actually have?
- How many do we use?
- How can we live within the budget that nature provides us?

Each time a country commits to operating within a one-planet budget, we all win.

MEET AN EXPERT!

Dr. Mathis Wackernagel

Co-creator of the Ecological Footprint
Executive Director, Global Footprint Network, United States

When Mathis was born, forty years ago, humanity used about half the planet's capacity. When his son was born in the year 2000, humans used about a planet and a quarter. By the time his son is Mathis's age, according to even the most conservative UN predictions, we will be using twice the planet's capacity. And that just has to change!

CAUTION:
NOT SAFE FOR KIDS OR YOUR UNCLE LOUIE...

You may have seen individual footprint calculators that invite you to measure your own footprint. But the thing is, it's really difficult to come up with a good score—using less than one planet's worth of resources—if you live in North American or European society as it is today. The ecological footprint concept is designed to help governments, corporations, and powerful people properly account for how heavily we live on the planet. It's up to them to break out the calculator and start putting in place the changes needed to get us down to the right size. The more important message for you personally is to start thinking about how heavily you live on the planet and to choose to change the five-planet norm.

The top five things Mathis thinks governments should commit to:

1. Be honest that there are ecological limits on Earth. We're using more than the planet can give us.

2. Establish the goal of one-planet living.

3. Keep accounts. Use tools, like the ecological footprint, to keep track of how much ecological credit we have and how fast we're going into ecological debt.

4. Tackle things that will last the longest first. Focus on building energy-efficient, carbon-neutral, sustainable cities with good public transit because once these infrastructures are built they take a very long time to change.

5. Drive all innovation toward winning the race against time to have people live sustainably on Earth.

Mathis's BIG three for individual one-planet living:

1. Gauge what you really need versus what you think you want.

2. Learn to be happy with what you have rather than trying to get more and more stuff.

3. Focus on the big items—like how energy efficient your home is, how you get to school, how often your family drives places—rather than worrying about every small, individual action you do.

Chapter Four
PEOPLE POWER
Energy that comes from you!

Just one...more...push. You're there! Take a moment to admire the view from the top of the hill. Oh no...is that the bell?

You point your bike toward your school and go! Bikes can get you places fast. And bike riding uses even less energy than walking. Thanks to safe bike lanes, steep taxes on cars, high gas prices, and a pro-bike attitude, people in Germany, Denmark, Colombia, and the Netherlands are many times more likely to ride a bike to school or work than Canadians and Americans. In Amsterdam, bikes recently edged out cars as the primary way that people travel in the city. Copenhagen provides 2,500 free bikes at 125 racks across the city, funded by advertising on the bikes.

Happily, pressure to make North American cities just as bike-friendly is succeeding. In San Francisco, for instance, thanks to improvements that make it cheaper, faster, and safer to ride, the number of people who choose to bike has doubled in just a couple of years. For the first time in decades, people in the United States and Australia are buying more bikes than cars. The bike revolution is changing the way we think of transportation around the world. More than twice as many bikes as cars will be built on Earth this year.

Not so very long ago, the city streets of China swarmed with bicycles. In fact, most of the bikes sold in North America are still made there. But in the past thirty years, cars have taken over the roads, bringing traffic congestion and stinky exhaust pollution. Now a brand-new love affair with bikes is sweeping China. E-bikes—electric bikes—are basically pedal-powered machines with an electric-powered motor to help you up hills. Chinese electric bikes number more than 100 million—that's four times the number of Chinese private cars!

It's all great news for people and the planet—and there's more good news to come. The people power that propels you on your bike has the potential to power the world in ways you never imagined. Architecture students in Massachusetts recently won an international competition for inventing a chair that transfers the power generated when someone sits down into enough energy to make four LED (light-emitting diode) lights shine. Scale up the idea to harness the bums on seats of thousands of baseball fans leaping up and down in the stands and you'd be able to light the stadium! Curious about green bike design or ways to power up your favorite dance music by tapping your toes? *Flip the page, baby!*

GROW YOUR OWN BIKE?

Here are my tomatoes, these are my roses, and over here—that's where my new bicycle is planted!

Can you lift your bike above your head? It isn't easy! Most bike frames are made from steel that is so strong and heavy, it's also used to hold up houses and skyscrapers! Steel is one of the most common materials in the world, and it's made from iron, the most common element in the Earth's crust. While it's true that bike riding is completely human-powered, it still takes lots of other kinds of energy to make a typical steel-framed bike. Electricity powers the giant drills and shovels that extract the iron ore, and diesel fuel runs the hauling trucks. Limestone—cut from a quarry and crushed—is needed to remove impurities from the iron. Coal—strip-mined from the Earth—heats the furnaces that transform the iron into steel. But what if you could skip all that and just grow bikes instead?

That's just what Craig Calfee is doing. He builds bikes from bamboo. Craig got the idea by watching his dog, Luna, try to gnaw a tough piece of bamboo growing behind his bike shop in Santa Cruz, California. He wondered if this incredibly fast-growing plant might be strong enough to become a bike. Ten years later, his company manufactures a hundred sleek bamboo racing bikes a year. He's also working with organizations in Ghana, Africa, to host bamboo bike-building workshops in poor communities where bamboo is plentiful enough for people to grow their own bikes.

Eats glass! Rides bikes! It's a giant panda?!

Bamboo is often called glass grass because it contains such a high concentration of silica—one of the main minerals in glass. You may think of glass as fragile, but thanks to silica, it's actually quite strong. That's why it breaks rather than bends, and why it's so difficult to scratch. Silica makes bamboo strong enough to be fashioned into a bike frame, but hard bamboo splinters would slice through the stomachs of most animals if they tried to eat it. With the aid of an incredibly slimy mucus lining in their guts, giant pandas can feast on shards of bamboo without injury. And there's another surprising connection to bikes—though breeding these endangered species is the top priority today, giant pandas riding tricycles starred in circuses in the past.

What would you use to build a green bike?

There are more options than just bamboo. Here are some recent examples of what green bike builders are experimenting with to get your creative juices flowing:

Cardboard? A twenty-one-year old British student created a cheap and fully recyclable bike from heavy-duty cardboard. Total cost? $30. Just don't leave it out in the rain!

Wood? About 150 years ago, antique bikes with wooden wheels gave such bumpy rides, they were called "boneshakers." The wooden bikes crafted by an Austrian design firm these days are so sleek, they'd spin circles around those older models.

Recyclable plastic? Remember the recyclable polypropylene used to make the fleece jackets on page 14? A young industrial designer in California used the same material to create a fully functioning recyclable bike.

A Battery? Twenty-three million electric bikes with battery-powered motors were sold worldwide in 2009, and the number is expected to double by 2012. Fans say that e-bikes are quiet, non-polluting, and create less traffic in crowded cities. Critics note they will be even better with an eco-friendly replacement for their current lead batteries.

And here's the compost pile for my bike helmet

Real bike riders love their helmets. If you crash and hit a hard surface, the foam part of your helmet crushes, controlling the crash energy and extending your head's stopping time by about six-thousandths of a second. That's enough to reduce the peak impact to your brain and to prevent about 85% of cyclists' head injuries. The skulls of dome-headed dinosaurs worked much the same way. When two pachycephalosaurus got combative and knocked heads, their skulls compressed and rebounded, preventing a brain bashing.

Bike helmet designers are hot on the green trend, too. You can download instructions from the internet to create a solar-powered helmet that charges batteries. The batteries power headlights to guide you home at night. An Italian helmet manufacturer recycles the steam used to expand the foam in their helmets back into heat for their buildings. Waste trimmings from the plastic shell of the helmets is ground into powder that becomes new plastic. So far, no one has come up with a helmet that could decompose in your compost heap. But with biodegradable foams and corn-based plastics becoming more common, the time is ripe to try. Put the criteria together—strong, lightweight, safe, attractive, compostable—and challenge yourself to design it!

HUMAN BEING, HUMAN DOING

People have energy to burn, and new technologies are transforming it in powerful ways.

Jump! Wiggle! Stomp! A new type of dance floor at a club in Rotterdam transforms the energy of the dancers themselves into electricity to run the light shows. Push the revolving doors in a train station in the Netherlands and you'll help light up the entrances. Hop on the exercise machines at a number of new green gyms and you can listen to music systems powered by you. Self-winding kinetic wristwatches recharge through the swinging movement of your arms as you walk. Yo-yo-styled ice cream makers whip up tasty treats with flicks of the wrist. Pedal-powered washing machines bring clean laundry and local jobs to villages in Peru. In many parts of the world, listening to the radio or shining a flashlight comes with turns of a crank.

And innovations like these are just the beginning. A new breed of personal energy harvesters and crowd farmers design ways to harness the green energy generated by human bodies. What kind of power are we talking about exactly? It's true that alone, one person isn't exactly much. A single step can power two 60-watt light bulbs for just one flickering second. But combine the energy from a crowd of 30,000 footsteps in that same second and there would be enough power to move a train. Now that's worth harnessing!

Imagine a world where our bodies or the things we do with them could power things in these exciting new ways. The technology is already in the works!

Feed the floodlights at ball stadiums from spectators climbing the staircases.

Run our MP3 players while we're walking with nanowires in the soles of our shoes.

Wear solar panels in our clothes to charge our batteries while we're playing in the sunshine.

Illuminate traffic lights through the vibrations produced from the cars we drive on the roads.

You are your own power plant...

When you walk quickly, you generate more than 60 watts of power. Tapping your finger creates 0.1 watt. Your breathing and arm movements each produce about one watt. Much of the energy conversion in your body, such as the vibrations of your vocal chords, occurs at a scale so incredibly tiny, researchers measure it in nanometers (one-millionth of a millimeter). Now researchers are creating tiny generators (nanogenerators) that use that energy to power devices inside the body. It might not be long before heart pacemakers and other medical devices run on electricity generated from the energy of your flowing blood.

And other animals are, too!

In 2009, researchers in Georgia fashioned a tiny hamster jacket equipped with nanowires and successfully captured energy generated by the tiny twists and movements of the animal spinning its wheel. Sure it's a tiny amount of energy, but the researchers say even the most minuscule of motions can produce electrical current. By using enough nanogenerators, engineers might eliminate the need for batteries in small handheld computers and other devices.

Of course, there are also those astonishing animals that actually produce power, like electric eels! If an eel wanted a hot meal, for example, it could generate enough electricity to power a microwave. Aquariums in Japan, Canada, and other places are putting that power to work, celebrating the holidays with an electric-eel-powered Christmas tree.

Elin Explains

HOW PENGUINS ARE CONNECTED TO YOUR BICYCLE

What happens on the streets is linked to the world's oceans. *Here's the scoop!*

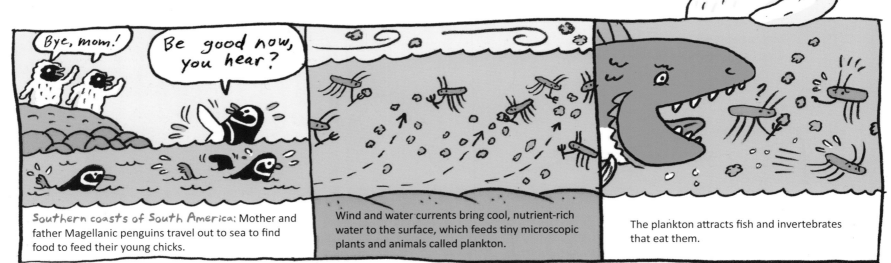

Bye, mom!

Be good now, you hear?

Southern coasts of South America: Mother and father Magellanic penguins travel out to sea to find food to feed their young chicks.

Wind and water currents bring cool, nutrient-rich water to the surface, which feeds tiny microscopic plants and animals called plankton.

The plankton attracts fish and invertebrates that eat them.

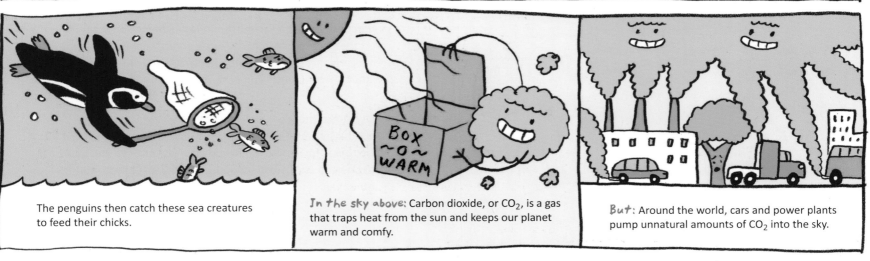

BOX ~O~ WARM

The penguins then catch these sea creatures to feed their chicks.

In the sky above: Carbon dioxide, or CO_2, is a gas that traps heat from the sun and keeps our planet warm and comfy.

But: Around the world, cars and power plants pump unnatural amounts of CO_2 into the sky.

The ocean waters get warmer because the extra CO_2 gas in the atmosphere traps more and more heat from the sun.

Climate change makes ocean productivity more variable. It's more difficult for Magellanic penguins to find food.

Scientists have found that if an adult penguin has to travel too far to find food, its chick could starve before it returns. Oh no!

Meanwhile: Governments rally behind seabirds and other ocean animals by designating places where humans can't fish. Like national parks on land, marine protected areas help conserve ocean habitats.

Your hometown: But wait, you and your bike can help out, too!

Bikes are the ultimate clean-air, zero-emission vehicles. They're good for your body and better for the environment because no gas is burned to power them—so no CO_2!

To encourage people to bike more, countries like Germany, Denmark, Colombia, and the Netherlands build many safe bike lanes and place steep taxes on cars.

In crowded Tokyo suburbs, bicycle parking towers use robotic arms to park the bikes of subway commuters. People pick their bikes up when they come home.

So next time you're on a bike, remember—penguins say thanks for helping to keep their water cooler!

YOUR BODY CAN POWER THE WORLD IN EVEN MORE SURPRISING WAYS

Ewwwww…pew…it may sound a little gross, but generating energy from poop and pee is no joke. It's really happening, and it's a great idea, too!

Biogas power is sweeping the planet. Large-scale plants in major European cities provide heat and electricity to thousands of homes, while family-sized biogas units are popping up in rural communities across Asia and Africa. Twenty million households in China get their cooking energy from biogas, and the government is working hard to increase that number. Biogas cars designed for the European market are rolling out of factories and speeding onto the roads—an Audi A4 recently set a new speed record for a biogas-converted race car: 365 kph (226 mph)!

Biogas from sewage and fish guts keeps buses on the road in Trollhattan, Norway.

Luten, Germany, is set to become the first community to integrate biogas throughout its city systems providing cheap, sustainable electricity and heat to about 25,000 residents.

The waste you flush down the toilet each year could create enough biogas to drive 120 km (75 miles). Poop naturally contains bacteria that releases methane—one of the heat-trapping gases linked to climate change.

A Rwandan prison won a global environmental award for generating its own power using methane gas from its toilet waste.

POOP XPRESS

POOP

BIO-HYDRO
POOP 2 POWER
2 FOR YOU!

Human waste powers streetlights in the Indian town of Thiruneermalai.

DUNG DINER

In India, machines called digesters convert the waste generated by a family of four into gas to cook their meals.

WE COOK WITH POOP!

DINNER LUNCH BREAKFAST

WELCOME!

heh heh

In Switzerland, the methane from more than 450 sewage treatment plants (pew!) is trapped to make biogas (yay!) that heats houses and powers city buses.

And your little dog, too

Folks in San Francisco are testing ways to turn little bags of doggie doo into fuel. One tonne (1.1 tons) of dog poop (pew!) will produce enough fuel to heat a house for two weeks. Imagine the power waiting to be unleashed by the 10 million tonnes (11 million tons) of cat and dog poop (super peeeew!) produced by pets in the United States this year.

Or even an elephant!

Zoos are the first to admit that they're in the poo-and-pee business. A single elephant, for example, produces around 200 kg (440 pounds) per day. From Toronto to Dallas to Copenhagen, zoos in major cities around the world are racing to generate more of their own power using dung from the exotic animals in their care.

But beware the farts and the belches

They look so cute and cuddly, but cows and sheep have a dark side. Sidle up to one on a farm and you'll get a whiff of the problem.

1 cow burps and farts out **90 to 180 kg (200 to 400 pounds) of methane** (another greenhouse gas) per year
x 1.5 billion cows + 1 billion sheep (that's how many live on Earth) + **DEFORESTATION** of rainforests to grow crops to feed them + **FOSSIL FUELS** to move them to market
= **MORE greenhouse gas** emissions than the **SUM of all cars, boats, and planes.**

Eating less meat, scientists say, like choosing to ride your bike, is a great way to keep you and the planet healthier.

57

GREENER WAYS TO LIGHT THE WORLD

Most of the electricity in the United States is generated from fossil fuels, such as coal, natural gas, and oil. When fossil fuels burn, they release CO_2 and other gases that contribute to climate change. The good news is that there are far greener ways to power our world out there. People living near Niagara Falls in Canada and the United States, for instance, have been lighting their homes and offices thanks to hydro-electric energy for many decades. These days, more governments are questioning the logic of using oil, gas, and coal technologies as "one size fits all" solutions and are looking to their own unique local environments for unique sources of power:

Volcanoes: Energy from hot rocks powers houses and restaurants, and provides the hot water that heats 95% of Iceland's homes. (Now that's hot.)

Water: Roughly 60% of the electricity produced in Canada comes from hydro-electric power.

Sun: Germany may have cloudy skies, but it generates more than half of the world's solar electricity. (Don't forget your sunscreen!)

Wind: One-fifth of Denmark's electricity comes from wind turbines, and Danes are working hard to raise the amount to 50%.

Tides: The year 2008 marked the first time tidal power was used to generate power for homes in Northern Ireland and Scotland, leading some to dub the United Kingdom "the Saudi Arabia of marine energy."

Nuclear: France produces so much electricity from its nuclear power stations, it exports 18% of it to other European countries.

French fry fuel: Thanks to a simple conversion kit that allows diesel cars to shift to vegetable oil, vehicles all over the world are revving up on the waste from fast food restaurants. (Ah, the power of a lowly potato.)

Alcohol: A Swedish train and more than a quarter of Stockholm's city buses run on alcohol confiscated at the border. Instead of pouring it down the drain (glug, glug), officials send it to a factory where it is mixed with water, sewage, and animal remains from meat-processing plants to create biogas. Sweden has pledged to become the first country not to use oil by 2020.

BRIGHT IDEAS

Say "night, night" to night lights

You might think that the lights that keep our cities bright at night would help migrating birds see where they are going. Unfortunately, many birds, especially young ones on their first migrations, are attracted to and confused by city lights. Millions end up colliding with skyscrapers (ouch!). Toronto and New York City provide safer passage for birds by dimming the lights in some office towers during migration. In a German village, residents leave the city dark, triggering the streetlights to shine when they need them using a code activated by their cell phones. By encouraging other cities to do similar things, we will spare millions of birds and save energy.

Can you please change the light bulb... when you finish university?

Like many families, you may be hanging colorful strings of LED holiday lights to guide Santa and his sleigh this year. LED bulbs can last for 30,000 hours or more, which means you may never have to change another red light on Rudolph's nose. Even if you left them shining for eight hours every day, LED bulbs can last ten years or more. Researchers at Purdue University recently discovered a new way to make LED bulbs as cheaply as compact fluorescent bulbs (CFLs). Once they hit the market, we'll have to get used to changing light bulbs every other decade.

Question: How many people does it take to change a light bulb?

Answer: Three hundred: One to hold the light bulb in place and 299 to spin the house!

Lately, lots of government leaders have been trying to solve the real-life riddle of how to change light bulbs. That's because ordinary light bulbs are real energy guzzlers. They waste 95% of electricity as heat and have barely changed since Thomas Edison first brought them to market 140 years ago. In 2007 Australia became the first country on Earth to ban the use of incandescent light bulbs. The European Union with its 500 million residents, as well as Canada and Argentina, has announced plans to do the same thing. At the beginning of 2009, more than forty countries had pledged to follow suit. If every American home replaces even one light bulb with a more energy-efficient CFL it will save enough energy to light more than 2.5 million homes for a year and prevent greenhouse gases equivalent to the emissions of nearly 800,000 cars. If everyone on Earth joins in, we will cut the world's lighting demand for electricity almost in half.

MEET A SUSTAINABLE HAPPINESS RESEARCHER

Dr. Catherine O'Brien

Cape Breton University, Canada

Imagine you are wandering through your ideal place to live. What does it look like? Sound like? Feel like? These are questions Dr. Catherine O'Brien thinks about a lot. She studies what makes people happy and how we can live in ways the Earth can sustain. She invited people all over the world to share their ideas about what makes a place delightful.

Here's what they said →

TOP TEN QUALITIES OF DELIGHTFUL PLACES:

1. A pleasure to walk or bike through
2. Peaceful
3. Beautiful
4. Appealing to kids, adults, and seniors
5. Lots of nature and green spaces
6. Welcoming
7. Lovely sounds of water, the wind, silence, people talking, and birds
8. The smell of earth, water, flowers, and food
9. A perfect place to relax
10. Endless opportunities to camp, canoe, garden, hike, swim, nap, or simply think

Catherine's Top Pick of a Delightful Sustainable Community:

"Barefoot College, Rajasthan, India, is a great example of a place that asked the question 'How can we completely revamp the education system so that we can sustain communities in this very poor region?' The entire campus is solar-powered. They harvest rainwater and grow organic food. Barefoot doctors bring care to the poorest of the poor in the region. Together they created a program that improves the well-being of people, communities, the environment, and the next generation."

Catherine is the first person to link the study of happiness with the study of how we can sustain the Earth. Here's how she defines this new field of research:

Sus·tain·a·ble happi·ness (noun)

1. Happiness that contributes to individual, community, and/or global well-being and does not exploit other people, the environment, or future generations.

Who is the happiest person you know?

Catherine asks her students to think of the happiest person they know and then sends them off to interview that person. Give yourself the same assignment. Chances are you'll discover that happiness doesn't come from being rich. It comes from loving relationships, meaningful activities, and having a genuine sense of purpose. That's good news for the planet because a big reason we are using up forests and rivers and oil so quickly is that people have been trying to buy happiness by acquiring more stuff—without success.

How do you study happiness when you're feeling grumpy?

It isn't easy! But Catherine says the more you study happiness, the more you notice when you're grumpy and you don't stay there. *"It doesn't feel great to be grumpy, but it's such a common experience for some people they don't even notice when they are,"* she says. *"They don't realize that it's a choice."*

Catherine's forecast for the decade ahead

Transportation engineers, the people who design how we travel around our cities, rarely think about how the placement of a road impacts how kids get around or whether its location will make more people happy. But these days, there's a growing concern about kids not getting enough exercise and suffering from obesity. Catherine sees more public health professionals attending transportation meetings and happiness research being applied to how we plan cities. In ten years' time, she believes more countries will be measuring the well-being of their citizens and the sustainability of their environments, through indexes such as Genuine Progress Index (GPI).

What makes you happy?

Walking in the rain? Tobogganing? Warm blankets? Snuggling with your dog? Watching a butterfly? Take time to notice and fill your life with delightful experiences.

When I grow up, I want to be rich!

That's a no-brainer, right? But is it true and what does being "rich" really mean? If it means having more money than others, then you're probably much wealthier than you realize. If your family makes more than $4,000 in a year, you are richer than 85% of the other people living on this planet. Almost half the world—more than 3 billion people—live on less than $2.50 a day.

According to a team of scientists at the University of British Columbia, giving money away actually makes you feel even happier than buying something for yourself. ♥

61

HAPPY PLANET, HAPPY LIFE

Kids all over the world have great ideas about how to live happy lives on a happy planet. Choosing a one-planet lifestyle that doesn't consume more than our fair share of the planet is a big part of the answer. And so is repairing the damage that's already been done. Every other year, nearly a thousand kids your age from more than a hundred countries gather to share their solutions for how to accomplish this. One of them is Felix Finkbeiner—he started Plant for the Planet Germany in 2008, when he was nine years old. By the end of 2009, thousands of children from over 500 schools around Germany had planted one million trees. His next goal is to plant one million trees in every country on Earth. But what really drives Felix is using people's interest in trees to raise awareness about more complicated subjects, such as climate justice and carbon-emission trading.

Old cities choose one-planet solutions...

Residents of Curitiba, Brazil, greened their city by planting 1.5 million trees. They solved the city's flood problems by diverting water into lakes in newly created parks. They pay the poor to keep the parks clean and reward people from squatter settlements who bring their trash in to be recycled with bus tickets or eggs, milk, oranges, or potatoes from local farms. Curitiba recycles two-thirds of its garbage—one of the highest rates of any city. Builders get a tax break if their projects include green areas. Bike paths and an efficient, well-used bus system connect the whole city.

And new communities do, too!

Brand-new communities, like BedZed in London, England, are also popping up around the globe. They're special places that use one-planet planning from the ground up, making sure that everything from the food on residents' plates to the location of their jobs is designed to be sustainable and not contribute greenhouse gases. The "world's largest eco-city," Masdar City, is under construction in the United Arab Emirates, and it promises to be the first zero-waste, zero-carbon city on Earth. By building high-density housing, where people live closer together in high-rise apartments and townhouses, for example, the city of Vancouver is reducing its ecological footprint and making it easier for people to walk to parks, child care, theaters, sport centers, and their jobs. Brave communities all over the globe are imagining what sustainable living looks like right on their own doorsteps, with very real and inspiring results!

What's your vision for living a happy life on a happy planet?

Human society changed more in the past century than in the previous ten thousand years thanks to the energy supplied by oil and gas. As oil supplies dwindle and worries about climate change and other environmental problems increase, you and your friends will create new visions about how to live in ways the Earth can support. Do you imagine the end of war and nuclear weapons? Or do you envision something simpler, like rows of vegetable gardens in place of front lawns? Or houses designed to be cooled by trees and heated by the sun rather than air conditioners and furnaces? How about new approaches to agriculture, where wild animals and farming flourishes?

What we dream and how we build it will have a tremendous impact on how our planet functions in the next century. By the time you're in your thirties, about half of the buildings in North America will have been built since you were born. China is building an entire America worth of homes, office buildings, and factories in the next twelve years. As Hal Harvey, a climate change expert, puts it, "Don't build stupid buildings: if we build energy-efficient communities like Copenhagen, Denmark, we win."

HOPEFUL ELIN, HOPEFUL YOU

I'm sorry to reach the end of this book because I loved writing it. But to be honest, I wasn't always happy when I was doing it. It's depressing to research the horrors of e-waste or plastic pollution. Yet I was also genuinely inspired. Positive changes are happening all over the planet. People change the world by building new technologies (remember all that power from poop!). Or they change the world by passing laws, like they're doing in the EU to reduce e-waste. Some, like Luke the local chef, lead change by example. Others develop new approaches, like the concept of ecological economics, to reframe the way we value the Earth. There are endless choices about how you and I and everyone else can create a happy life for ourselves and millions of other species. Ride a bike. Share stuff. Play outside. Eat less meat. Be silly. Play more. Choose an issue and commit to changing it, even if it's just a little. Recycle cell phones. Keep playing. **Reduce. Reimagine. Rejoice!**

Elin's tips for staying hopeful

- Give yourself lots of time to imagine, create, and play
- Learn as much as you can...and do it again the next day!
- Try to live a one-planet life and ask your family and friends to help you
- Be as kind to yourself as you would be to a friend
- When you feel sad celebrate the things you love
- Speak out for what you care about and be proud of yourself for being brave

Index

A

alternative energy 18, 25, 49, 50, 51, 52, 53, 55, 56, 57, 58, 59, 60
animals 5, 8, 9, 15, 21, 22, 23, 25, 30, 32, 37, 38, 39, 42, 44, 45, 46, 50, 53, 54, 55, 57, 63

B

bacteria 33, 41, 56
bamboo 8, 50
batteries 18, 51, 52, 53
bees 9, 24, 31, 32, 33
bikes 29, 49, 55
biodiversity 23, 45
biogas 56, 57, 58
biomimicry 18, 19
birds 9, 15, 22, 23, 25, 45, 55, 59, 60

C

carbon dioxide 46, 54, 55, 58
carbon emissions 9
cars 9, 38, 39, 44, 49, 52, 54, 55, 56, 57, 58, 59
cell phones 13, 41
CFLs 59
chemicals 7, 8, 9, 11, 18, 19, 23, 25, 33, 40
cities 21, 24, 25, 26, 35, 47, 49, 51, 56, 57, 59, 61, 62
clothing 7, 18, 29
coltan 42, 43

compost 51
computers 37, 41, 42, 43, 46, 53
cotton 7, 8, 9, 10, 11
crops 8, 9, 21, 22, 23, 24, 28, 32, 57

E

ecological footprint 31, 46, 47, 62
ecosystems 23
energy 9, 15, 18, 41, 46, 47, 49, 50, 51, 52, 53, 56, 58, 59, 63
e-waste 41

F

fabrics 7, 8, 10, 11, 19
farming 9, 22, 23, 24, 25, 27, 33, 63
fertilizers 8, 22
fish 13, 15, 22, 25, 29, 31, 38, 44, 54, 55, 56
food 7, 11, 12, 13, 15, 16, 21, 22, 23, 24, 25, 26, 27, 28, 29, 30, 31, 32, 33, 34, 39, 45, 46, 54, 55, 58, 60, 62
forest 12, 18, 25, 28, 29, 39
fossil fuels 21, 22, 23, 58

G

garbage 16, 37, 62
gas 49, 54, 55, 56, 57, 58, 63
gorillas 5, 42, 43

I

industrial agriculture 22, 23
insects 5, 8, 22, 23, 28, 31

J

jobs 28, 40, 41, 52, 62

L

LED 49, 59
local foods 26, 27

M

maps 22, 29, 44, 46
medicines 30
migration 59
money 7, 23, 28, 29, 41, 61

O

oceans 17, 38, 39, 44, 45, 54
oil 7, 8, 15, 21, 35, 58, 61, 63
organic 9, 23

P

paper 10
pesticides 8, 22, 33
petroleum 22
planet 4, 5, 7, 8, 18, 21, 22, 28, 29, 35, 37, 39, 44, 45, 46, 47, 49, 54, 56, 57, 61, 62, 63
plants 5, 9, 18, 23, 24, 25, 30, 32, 33, 39, 54, 56, 57, 58
plastic 14, 15, 16, 17, 51, 63
plastic bottles 14, 15
power 5, 8, 32, 49, 51, 52, 53, 54, 55, 56, 57, 58, 63
public transit 47

R

rainforests 25, 42, 46, 57
recycling 10, 14, 15, 17, 41, 43, 51, 62, 63
researchers 5, 19, 29, 33, 38, 39, 45, 47, 53, 60
resources 28, 46, 47

S

satellites 38, 44
sea lions 13
seals 13, 38, 45
seaweed 30, 31
shoes 17, 18, 29, 31, 52
soil 9, 16, 18, 23, 24, 46

T

transportation 49, 61
trees 15, 18, 23, 24, 25, 39, 62, 63

V

vegetables 11, 24, 30
video games 39, 40

W

waste 11, 15, 16, 17, 28, 37, 40, 41, 56, 57, 58, 59, 62, 63
water 8, 9, 11, 14, 19, 22, 23, 25, 28, 29, 34, 35, 38, 44, 45, 46, 54, 55, 58, 60, 62
whales 13, 21, 37, 38, 39, 45

Elin wishes to thank the dozens of scientists who kindly shared their knowledge in the creation of this book. Special thanks to the wonderful folks at the Writers' Trust of Canada and Berton House where this book was born. Thanks also to the talented professionals at Owlkids Books, the clever people at the Monterey Bay Aquarium, the hopeful people at Worldchanging.com, and all those clever kids at Robert Down School. Hugs to Andy, Kip, and Esmé for great ideas and constant inspiration.

[13]